GRAPHICS FOR PRESENTERS
Getting Your Ideas Across

Lynn Kearny

A FIFTY-MINUTE™ SERIES BOOK

CRISP PUBLICATIONS, INC.
Menlo Park, California

GRAPHICS FOR PRESENTERS
Getting Your Ideas Across

Lynn Kearny

CREDITS
Managing Editor: **Kathleen Barcos**
Editor: **Colleen Wilder**
Typesetting: **ExecuStaff**
Cover Design: **Carol Harris**
Artwork: **Lynn Kearny**

Copyright © 1996 by Lynn Kearny

Printed in the United States of America by Bawden Printing Company.

Distribution to the U.S. Trade:

National Book Network, Inc.
4720 Boston Way
Lanham, MD 20706
1-800-462-6420

http://www.crisp-pub.com

Library of Congress Catalog Card Number 94-68301
Kearny, Lynn
Graphics for Presenters
ISBN 1-56052-315-8

This book is printed on recyclable paper with soy ink.

LEARNING OBJECTIVES FOR:

GRAPHICS FOR PRESENTERS

The objectives for *Graphics for Presenters* are listed below. They have been developed to guide you, the reader, to the core issues covered in this book.

Objectives

❏ **1) To explain how to create visuals simply.**

❏ **2) To give tips on how to use visuals effectively.**

❏ **3) To discuss planning and handling visuals.**

Assessing Your Progress

In addition to the Learning Objectives, Crisp, Inc. has developed an **assessment** that covers the fundamental information presented in this book. A twenty-five item, multiple choice/true-false questionnaire allows the reader to evaluate his or her comprehension of the subject matter. An answer sheet with a summary matching the questions to the listed objectives is also available. To learn how to obtain a copy of this assessment please call: **1-800-442-7477** and ask to speak with a Customer Service Representative.

ABOUT THE AUTHOR

Lynn Kearny is an author, teacher, trainer and consultant with 20 years' experience, specializing in solving human performance problems through work-system improvement and training programs. In addition to being an award-winning instructional designer, co-winner of the NSPI Outstanding Instructional Product Award, she instructs other presenters how to use graphics more effectively through her workshop called "Graphics for Presenters." In another workshop, "Thinking with Groups," she has assisted in training hundreds of participants to successfully work with and lead their own groups through creative decision making processes for today's workforce and its demands.

ABOUT THE SERIES

With over 200 titles in print, the acclaimed Crisp 50-Minute™ series presents self-paced learning at its easiest and best. These comprehensive self-study books for business or personal use are filled with exercises, activities, assessments, and case studies that capture your interest and increase your understanding.

Other Crisp products, based on the 50-Minute books, are available in a variety of learning style formats for both individual and group study, including audio, video, CD-ROM, and computer-based training.

PREFACE

If you ever present ideas and information to other people, this book will show you how to have a greater impact and get better results by using simple graphics.

Why Use Graphics?

When you present information to others, is it important that they understand quickly and remember the details? If you're talking to a group, does it matter if they all have the same understanding of what you said?

Graphics present information visually, and people think visually. Did you know there are over *seven times* as many human brain cells devoted to visual processing as there are to hearing and touch? Even people who do not feel they are very visually-oriented have the same brain cells. Both practical experience and scientific research (in educational psychology and cognitive psychology) show that most people take in information faster, interpret it more accurately, and remember it better if they get it in a visual form.

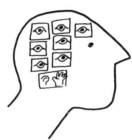

Think back to your early grade-school classrooms. Chances are you remember few specifics from your textbooks, but you probably remember the alphabet above the chalkboard, the map on the wall, and where any windows were. If you remember any of the books, you are likely to remember the pictures on the pages before you recall any words that went with them.

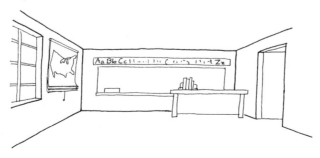

PREFACE (continued)

People also *enjoy* graphics. Pictures and color attract attention and hold people's interest. Look at the front page of any daily newspaper. What grabs your attention first? The big bold headlines and any pictures, especially if they are in color.

What If You Aren't an Artist?

If graphics (visual messages) will do all these things, why isn't everyone who has to communicate using them? Most people think you have to be an artist to do it, and they feel that if they aren't artists they shouldn't try. This is like thinking that if you aren't a professional like Bobby Unser, the race car driver, you shouldn't take a car on the road.

You can't get very far thinking that way. A simple flier or a classroom flip chart is not the Indy 500 of communications. You can create simple graphics with nothing but the alphabet and a few colored felt pens. Then you can stretch a little to draw a few simple icons, and have graphics your audience will find useful and enjoyable . . . even if you have no talent at all.

Does this mean you can create graphics without being able to draw? Of course you can! Thousands of people do it every day, and this book will show you how. It will give you all the skills you need to quickly create simple and inexpensive graphics that will help your audience get your message and remember it.

What Are Graphics?

In this book, a *graphic* is a tool using words, shapes, pictures, color and blank space together in some combination. Some graphics use no colors but black, gray and white. Look at newspaper ads. Other graphics have no pictures, just colors, shapes and interesting lettering. Look at posters and packaging.

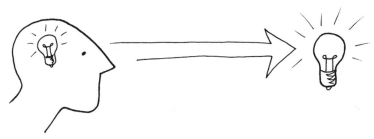

The purpose of a graphic is to get a message across to someone else. It could be conveyed in print, on a computer screen, on a slide or any other way of showing information to people. It must grab people's attention and get the idea across before they look away, so it must be brief and clear. This book will show you how.

Who Should Use This Book?

Anyone whose success depends on getting ideas and information across to others should use this book. Here are a few of the tasks these techniques can help you do better:

- Training
- Teaching
- Presentations
- Status Reporting
- Re-engineering
- Documentation
- Newsletters
- Fliers
- Posters

PREFACE (continued)

Results You Can Expect

If You Are a Beginner

This book will show you how to create simple graphics that will help you get your message across to most audiences. It begins at the level where most people are: using mostly print and maybe some color. It will take you step by step through new techniques, each time building on skills you already have.

All the techniques in this book can be done on paper with colored felt pens, because they are cheap, easy to use and available to most people.

You will learn how to:

- Use color effectively
- Use words and letters as graphics
- Use lines, borders and shapes
- Use a "graphic alphabet" to create simple pictures
- Use simple pictures to convey ideas (no talent needed)
- Think up the pictures
- Use focus and balance
- Get special effects
- Plan a series of visuals to support a presentation

You will *not* learn how to produce a highly polished and professional graphic, like an ad to be printed in a glossy magazine, a screen for a nationally-marketed software package or a slide show for a presentation to your stockholders. For that kind of work, you need to hire a graphics professional. However, even if that's what you're doing, you can use the techniques in this book to sketch out your ideas and help the graphic artist understand the message you want to get across.

If You Are Experienced

If you already use a lot of graphics in your work, this book should give you additional ideas to try. Be sure to look at the advanced techniques at the end. Try using multicolored borders, fancy lettering, depth, and hot or cold effects. Try using thumbnails to plan a long presentation before you invest time, energy and materials in full-sized visuals. Try "chunking" complex, wordy material and adding images to clarify the meaning of the chunks.

Graphics on Computers

If you work on a computer and have access to a scanner, it is probably easiest to draw images on paper first and scan them in, then edit or manipulate them on-screen. Most illustrators who use computers work this way. Freehand drawing on a computer is still awkward and consumes a lot of time, patience and computer memory. Most ideas and techniques in this book will still apply if you are working on-line. Color guidelines for screens are very different; for these see William Horton's book, listed in the bibliography.

Supplies You Will Need

You can do everything in this book with the following supplies:

EITHER	OR
• An unlined pad of flip-chart paper	• A handful of unlined $8^1/_2 \times 11$ paper
• A set of water-based felt-tipped colored markers in these colors:	• A set of fine-tipped colored felt pens (same colors)

green	brown
blue	red
turquoise	orange
purple	yellow

(Mr. Sketch™ 12-color set is best)

• A large blue highlighter pen (like Major Accent™)	• A small blue highlighter pen

(You can find a more detailed supply list with ideas for plastic charts, special effects and other goodies in the appendix.)

If you plan to make overhead transparencies, read about them on the following page.

PREFACE (continued)

This Is a Hands-On Book!

Be prepared to roll up your sleeves and try everything out as you go through the book. No one ever learned to drive a car by just reading a book; you have to get behind the wheel and try it yourself. Graphics is like that, too. Fortunately it's a lot of fun. So take your colored pens and paper, and let's get started. If you still worry about whether you have the talent, read page 3 and then get out your colored pens and paper.

If You Want to Make Overhead Transparencies

Most people will want to make transparencies using a presentation graphics computer program like PowerPoint™. I love these programs, but there are some pitfalls to watch out for. I recommend you use plain white paper and colored pens to plan your graphics first, keeping them plan and simple. Then use the computer program to help you jazz them up and produce the final transparencies.

If you start with the program, it's easy to be drawn into the gizmos and distracted by all the clip art images available. At this point, your computer program is using you, rather than the other way around. It's easy to end up with a bunch of jazzy-looking slides that don't really help the audience understand your ideas quickly and remember them.

Other Options for Creating Overhead Transparencies

- Use a word processing program with a variety of large outline fonts and some very simple cartoon-like clip art you can color in with overhead transparency pens. Please consider drawing your own images on paper and scanning them in. It's hard to find clip art images that really do what you want them to do.

This is a large outline font

- Hand letter and draw on your overheads with colored permanent overhead pens. I use this approach a lot, but you must be very careful to use neat lettering. I use graph paper under the transparency to help. The best pens I have found are Staedtler Lumocolor™ AV markers with medium, broad and extra broad tips. The fine tip makes lines too small to be read easily by your audience. Staedtler also has the largest selection of colors I have found in overhead pens, though unfortunately there are only eight. Be sure to get their correction pen for removing errors. Q-Tips™ are also useful for removing errors.

CONTENTS

PART 1   INTRODUCTION 1

PART 2   USES FOR GRAPHICS 5

PART 3   WORDS AND LETTERS 11

PART 4   LINES AND GEOMETRIC SHAPES 19

PART 5   COLOR 25

PART 6   SIMPLE PICTURES 33

PART 7   PUTTING IT ALL TOGETHER 49

PART 8   COMPOSITION 55

PART 9   PLANNING A PRESENTATION 65

PART 10   ADVANCED TECHNIQUES 83

PART 11   MORE ON MATERIALS 99

PART 12   BIBLIOGRAPHY 107

P A R T

1

Introduction

WELCOME TO GRAPHICS FOR PRESENTERS, THE NO-TALENT GUIDE TO GOOD VISUAL AIDS

First, a Word On Talent

Talent is defined as "a natural strength or ability." People with a talent do something right and do it well. They often don't even know why they're doing it that way—they just do it because it seems right.

Talent is *not* the only way to do something well.

Next, a Word On Skill and Knowledge

Knowledge is knowing what's right. In the case of graphics, it's having a set of principles and guidelines to follow. You use them to create something, or to analyze and evaluate something to make it better.

Skill is having a set of techniques you can use to put your knowledge into action. Then you practice those techniques until you have some degree of confidence and facility. We're not talking about drill, here. This isn't musical scales or basketball practice. It just means to keep on doing graphics (flip charts, computer graphics, doodling or whatever) on a regular basis. If you only do it once a year, of course your efforts will feel awkward and rusty. But you can still do a good job, even if you only use graphics occasionally.

Back to Talent

Most people with talent practice a lot, too, but they may not know they're practicing. They think they're just having fun. They are on the right track. You'll always do something better if you have fun with it. Approach graphics playfully, and don't take your attempts too seriously. Remember this is a disposable flip chart, not the Sistine Chapel.

WELCOME TO GRAPHICS FOR PRESENTERS, THE NO-TALENT GUIDE TO GOOD VISUAL AIDS (continued)

You Have the Key Talent Already

As long as you can look at a page, a slide, or a flip chart and say "There's something wrong with that, but I'm not sure just what it is," you have the most important talent for this kind of work.

Now all you need is skill and knowledge.

P A R T

2

Uses for Graphics

USING VISUAL AIDS

This book will show you how to use words, color, shapes, pictures and blank space to create a visual aid. The picture can be very simple, like an icon or a symbol. The visual aid can be anything from a flip chart to a flier, as long as it helps people to learn. This means we will be using graphics to do a real job, not just to decorate. Here are some ways you can put graphics to work:

Use pictures and symbols to evoke:

- Ideas

- Feelings

- Attitudes and values

- Facts

- Events

- Sequences

Feelings

Attitudes, Values

As a presenter, you can use graphics to do all these things. Some specific applications are to:

- ▶ Present and review key ideas

- ▶ Develop important images

  - metaphors and analogies (for example, building a career is like building a house)

  - themes (for example, "invest time")

- ▶ Give instructions

  - forms and procedures

  - exercises

- ▶ Keep yourself on track (visual clues for the presenter)

- ▶ Enliven dry material with visual elements, such as cartoons or bright colors

USING VISUAL AIDS (continued)

Examples:

Key Idea

Instructions

Stay on Track

Graphic elements that are quick and easy to use are:

- Words and letters (plus *blank* space!)
- Lines and geometric shapes
- Color
- Simple pictures (icons)

Examples:

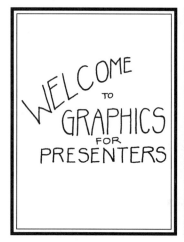

Words & Letters

Words, Lines & Shapes

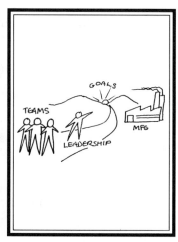

Simple Pictures

The next few sections of the book will give you the basic techniques for using all of these graphic elements.

Words and Letters (Plus Blank Spaces) will give you some guidelines for using words graphically, so they're easy to read. The key is to use lots of blank space on the page.

Lines and Geometric Shapes can be added to direct attention and clarify meaning. They're also very easy to use, so this is a short section.

Color is a great attention-grabber and a lot of fun to use. This section will give you guidelines for working with color. The color section should ideally come first, but you need something to practice with, so we'll use this opportunity to review and practice the last two sections.

Simple Pictures can be made from basic geometric shapes, which act like an alphabet for drawing. We won't even try to do complicated "realistic" drawing. We'll use symbolic drawing instead: simple, icon-like pictures that are fast and easy to draw and to understand.

Then you'll get some practice putting them all together in one visual aid, either a flip chart or an overhead transparency.

PART

3

Words and Letters

WELCOME TO GRAPHICS FOR PRESENTERS

GUIDELINES FOR WORDS AND LETTERS

Words (and the letters that make them up) are the most important graphic element we have for communicating ideas and information.

Books, newspapers, even computer screens deliver most of the information using printed words. From reading books we have gotten used to seeing words packed closely together, but that isn't always the best way to communicate important information. When a page is tightly packed with print, it takes a while to read it and decide what's key and what's just supporting information. Not everyone will read and interpret it the same way. When speed and consistency are important, you need to arrange the words on the page so people can grasp the key ideas quickly and so everyone will get the same message. Fliers, instructions, summaries and visual aids are some of those situations requiring speed and consistency.

Here are some simple guidelines for using words and letters effectively on hand-lettered flip charts:

Guidelines

► PRINT IN CAPS $1^1/_2$" HIGH

► ALTERNATE COLORS

► USE ONLY KEY WORDS

► LIST NO MORE THAN 5 IDEAS/PAGE

► LEAVE LOTS OF WHITE SPACE

THE GUIDELINES IN DETAIL

Print in capital letters 1 to $1\frac{1}{2}$ inches high if you are doing hand-lettered flip charts. The larger the audience, the larger your printing should be. Try making one test sheet and looking at it from the same distance as the farthest participant will be in your class.

If you are hand lettering, use only capitals unless your handwriting is as neat as a typewriter and your small (lower-case) letters are very large. Most people's small letters quickly degenerate into a tiny, illegible scrawl.

> **Note:** If you are preparing slides or overheads on a computer, upper- and lower-case letters are fine, but be sure you use at least a 36-point font and follow the next four guidelines carefully.

Alternate Colors with Each Idea

If you wrote the first idea in blue, write the second idea in another color, like brown. Keep alternating the same two colors throughout the flip chart. This helps your audience separate the ideas easily and makes the sheet more legible. To see how this works, use two colored felt pens and copy the short version of these guidelines (in the box on the previous page) as if you were going to present them to a class. Can you see the difference?

Avoid using lots of colors to letter the same sheet: it can be confusing and distracting. We'll add more color guidelines in the section on color.

> **Note:** If you are using a computer program to create a slide show, you do not need to alternate colors to separate ideas. The software will give you other options for accomplishing the same result.
>
> If you are using a word processor to create overhead transparencies, use an outline font and color in the letters with overhead pens.

Use Key Words Only

Avoid the compulsion to write complete sentences. Avoid the temptation to add interesting tidbits. Remember, your purpose is to help people grasp the key idea quickly: give them a visual aid they can scan quickly while you elaborate, either in your presentation or (if this is a page in a manual) in accompanying text. The short version of these guidelines (shown previously) is a good example of this.

Maximum of Five Ideas Per Page

Research has shown that the average person can only hold about five ideas (or "chunks" of meaningful information) in his or her working memory at one time. Above five, the person starts to lose track. Since our purpose is to help people understand faster and remember better, why make them lose track? If you have a list of ten basic steps, break them into two lists and present only five at a time. Inevitably, you will sometimes break this guideline. Just be aware that you're breaking it, and do something else to compensate for it (like using pictures or reviewing more often).

Note: If you are creating slides, limit information to one idea per slide. When you are showing visuals in a darkened room, you need to change the visual more frequently to keep people awake.

Leave Lots of Blank Space

Leave a lot of empty space or "air" around the words and pictures in your graphics. It makes the sheet easier to scan quickly and comprehend. The space lets the ideas breathe, which helps bring them to life. The more stuff there is in a graphic, the harder it is to read, understand and remember.

COMMON MISTAKES

Here are some of the most common mistakes people make while using words in a visual aid:

► Making an overhead transparency of a page of text. The audience can rarely even read it, let alone understand it. A computer screen that's solid text is also a big mistake.

► Putting too many ideas on one sheet or screen.

► Putting too much of anything on one sheet; such as words, pictures and colors.

► Failing to leave enough blank space for the ideas to "breathe."

► Making the print too small for the audience to read.

► Failing to use bullets to show where a new point begins.

► Showing the same slide for too long in a darkened room while the audience quietly dozes off.

USING THE GUIDELINES

Here are some things to do to put these guidelines to work for you:

1. If you haven't already done so, pick two colored pens and a piece of blank paper and reproduce the "Guidelines" flip chart from page 13, as if it were a visual aid you were going to present to a class. Then imagine the full text explanation above, reproduced as an overhead transparency.

► If you were sitting in a classroom, which would be easier for you to understand quickly and remember?

► If you copied the guidelines as a full-sized flip chart, tape it to a wall and look at it from a distance. How far away could a participant sit and still read it easily?

► Is your printing clear and legible? If not, try using flip-chart paper with one-inch grid lines, and copy it again more clearly. To make your lettering bold and clear, look at the tip of your felt pen. If it has a chisel tip, one side will be wider. Use this wide side to make your letters. If you have a bullet-tipped marker, try using a chisel-tipped one instead.

2. Find a flip chart or other visual aid you have been using in a class or presentation. Analyze it using the guidelines.

► Which guidelines does it seem to follow?

► Which guidelines (if any) does it ignore?

► If it missed any guidelines, take fresh paper and two colors of pens and re-do it again, according to the guidelines. Do you think the new version will be easier to understand or remember? Why or why not?

3. Pick something you will have to present soon (or have presented recently) and find at least one important part that you want people to understand quickly, interpret consistently and remember.

► Take a fresh paper and two colored felt pens or markers and use the guidelines to create a visual aid. If you are presenting more than one idea on a sheet, use bullet points.

USING THE GUIDELINES (continued)

►   Review your work using the list of common mistakes above, and correct anything you don't like. To correct a flip-chart page, you can:

   • paint out small errors with pen and ink white-out

   • tape and write over wrong words with Post-It™ correction tape (1 inch)

   • re-do the flip chart quickly by tracing it with a fresh sheet

►   If your visual is a flip chart, tape it to the wall and decide whether the lettering is big enough that the whole audience can read it easily, or if you will need to re-do it as an overhead transparency. An overhead transparency can be projected much larger than a flip chart.

4

Lines and Geometric Shapes

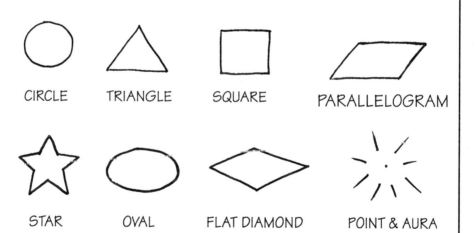

CIRCLE   TRIANGLE   SQUARE   PARALLELOGRAM

STAR   OVAL   FLAT DIAMOND   POINT & AURA

SHAPES AND LINES

By now you should be comfortable using the guidelines for words and letters, and be ready for some new techniques. The simplest things to add are lines and geometric shapes. They're easy to use and can do a lot to make a page easier to read and more interesting to look at.

Lines

I use lines for two main purposes:

1. To separate large chunks of information on a page or chart, especially if I don't have enough blank space to create the separation.

Examples:

WORKPLACE FEATURES

PHYSICAL

- FIXED
- NOT FIXED
- VISIBLE

SENSORY

- CONTROLLABLE
- NOT CONTROLLABLE
- NOT VISIBLE

MENTAL WORKLOAD
(Attention Demand)

TYPES OF MENTAL WORK
- ROUTINE
- COMPLEX

SCREENING BEHAVIORS
- HIGH SCREENER
- LOW SCREENER

SHAPES AND LINES (continued)

2. To create colorful borders for important flip charts or overhead transparencies, like cover sheets, objectives and agendas. Borders are also useful for fliers and important handout pages. They make the page stand out from borderless sheets.

Examples:

Try making the borders in different colors that look good together. Some combinations I use are:

- A dark blue outside, a turquoise border inside, and dark blue letters.

- A light-green border outside, an orange border inside, and dark green letters.

You Try It

Take the visual aid you did for practice with words and letters, and add colored borders that you think will go well with the colors you used for lettering.

> **TIP:** Always use at least one of the colors you used for lettering to make one of the borders.

> **TIP:** Adding a thin inside border with a hot color (red, orange, fuchsia) looks great and really attracts attention.

You can use the blank space below and some fine-tipped colored felt pens to experiment.

Geometric Shapes

Here are two good uses for geometric shapes:

1. Make bullets that direct attention. Anytime you are presenting a list, bullets make it easy for the viewer to scan the items quickly. Avoid numbering the items because the numbers just blend in and give the viewer more to read and interpret. Compare these examples:

Unmarked list	Numbered list	Bulleted list
WORKPLACE STRESS SIGNALS ADAPTATION LOW ENERGY AVOIDANCE EMOTIONALITY ILLNESS/INJURY	WORKPLACE STRESS SIGNALS 1. ADAPTATION 2. LOW ENERGY 3. AVOIDANCE 4. EMOTIONALITY 5. ILLNESS/INJURY	WORKPLACE STRESS SIGNALS • ADAPTATION • LOW ENERGY • AVOIDANCE • EMOTIONALITY • ILLNESS/INJURY

SHAPES AND LINES (continued)

Here are some shapes to use for bullets:

2. As building blocks for simple pictures that take no talent to draw. We will go into that right after the section on color.

You Try It

Take the visual aid you did for practice with lettering and colored borders. If there is more than one idea on it, add bullet points.

> **TIP:** Hot colored bullets look great. If you already used a hot color for a border, use the same one for the bullets.

> **TIP:** Fat triangles tipped on edge look like an arrowhead and are very effective for directing attention. *Example:* ▶

5

Color

Face
Front

Lively
Profile

Self-Satisfied

Distressed

WHY USE COLOR?

Color does a lot of useful things to help communicate information:

First, it attracts people's attention. Hotter, brighter colors attract attention more, and cooler, darker colors attract it less. You can use this rule to direct where people look on graphics you create.

Second, people tend to relate similar colors (like blue and turquoise) and separate colors that are different (like green and brown). You can use this in your graphics to help people relate similar ideas by color coding them. For example, you can write similar items in blue and turquoise or in dark green and bright green. You can also help keep ideas separate by writing them in unrelated colors, like purple and brown. We used that principle when we alternated colors with each idea in the guidelines for words and letters: it helps people see that the ideas are separate.

Third, color can help people learn what something looks like so they can recognize it again. It is much more effective to show someone a colored picture of a highway sign or a traffic light than to tell them what it looks like in words. People often need to recognize and discriminate items by color for their job. For example, color codes show the resistance of a transistor. This makes color an important part of technical training and documentation.

Fourth, most people like color and simply enjoy the presentation more if you use it. This makes them much more likely to pay attention and to remember what you said.

WHAT YOU NEED TO KNOW ABOUT COLOR AND VISUAL AIDS

The color recommendations in this book are mainly for paper flip charts and overhead transparencies made with a clear white or pale-colored background. They will also work fine for printed paper, but printing in color is still very expensive and not many organizations will pay for it. Unless you have a large budget I suggest you create graphics for manuals, newsletters or handouts that work with black, white and grayscale rather than relying on color to carry your design. The exception is a technical manual or job aid in which people need to recognize something by color to do the work correctly.

If you are designing graphics for a computer screen, you should research and follow recommendations created for that industry. William Horton's book *Illustrating Computer Documentation* is a good source (see bibliography for details).

If you are creating 35mm slides to be projected in a dark room, follow the color recommendations that come with your presentation graphics computer software. I suggest you limit the colors on a single slide to two main "cool" colors and one "hot" color for emphasis until you have a lot of experience combining colors. Don't worry about the colors in your clip art—they should be fine.

If you use a software package to create overhead transparencies, I strongly recommend you stick with clear white or very pale-colored backgrounds for your overheads. The deep vibrant blue and other colored backgrounds do look gorgeous when you hold them up to the light. However, if you project them in a lighted room where people are writing and referring to printed materials, reflected light from the room may cause your beautiful deep-colored overheads to pale out and become almost illegible.

COLOR BASICS

On the following pages are some guidelines for using color, along with some coloring-book style job aids for using and combining colors. Color the little boxes in with your felt pens so you can see the colors and how they work together.

Cool Colors

Use two cool colors for text on each page. Cool colors are calm and relaxing for most people. For this reason, use mainly cool colors for your graphics, especially text.

The cool colors are:

☐ Blue   ☐ Dark Green

☐ Turquoise   ☐ Bright Green

☐ Purple   ☐ Black

☐ Brown

Hot Colors

Use hot colors sparingly: one or two key words, bullets points or special effects.

Hot colors are exciting and stimulating for most people, and really grab attention. For this reason, use them for emphasis *only*. Never use hot colors for text (other than one or two key words on a page).

The hot colors are:

☐ Fuchsia

☐ Orange

☐ Red

COLOR BASICS (continued)

Highlighter Colors

Use highlighters pens for borders, solid color areas, shading and other special effects. Highlighters are soft pale colors that are useful for special effects. They have just enough color strength to add interest without grabbing attention. Never use highlighters for text or the outline of an image, they are too pale to read.

The highlighter colors are:

- [ ] Yellow

- [ ] Blue Highlighter

- [ ] Purple Highlighter

- [ ] Green Highlighter

- [ ] Orange Highlighter

- [ ] Light Brown (you can use a dried-out brown felt pen diluted with injected water)

COMBINING COLORS

- Use three colors on each page: two cool colors for text and one hot color for emphasis.

- You can count dark blue and turquoise together as one cool or as two, whichever you wish. The same goes for dark green and bright green.

- You can use highlighters (especially yellow) without counting them as extra colors, however they look best with related colors, i.e., purple highlighter with a purple marker and so on.

- If you are adding simple drawings to your chart, either use realistic colors (i.e., brown people, green leaves) or use the two cool colors you used for text.

- If you are unsure what color combinations will look good together, use the chart on the next page as a guide. But don't treat the guide as a set of rules that can't be broken—use it as a source of inspiration.

To Coordinate With . . .	Use . . .	To Emphasize . . .
☐ Brown	☐ Purple or ☐ Green	☐ Orange
☐ Purple	☐ Blue or ☐ Green	☐ Red (or fuchsia, pink)
☐ Blue	☐ Purple or ☐ Brown	☐ Red (or fuchsia, pink)
☐ Green	☐ Blue or ☐ Brown	☐ Orange

USING THE COLOR GUIDELINES

Here are some things you can do to put these guidelines to work for you:

1. Pick another of the visual aids you created when you were practicing the guidelines for words and letters. Re-do it using the following:

- **Colors:** brown and purple for lettering, orange for bullets and one border

- **Bullets**

- **Borders:** at least two, one inside and one outside

2. Find other visual aids you would like to improve: maybe some black and white overhead transparencies or some flip charts done in only one color of felt pen. Try each of these color combinations:

- Purple, turquoise and orange

- Dark green, light green and orange

- Purple, dark blue and red

P A R T

6

Simple Pictures

WHY USE PICTURES?

If you want people to quickly, accurately and consistently understand what you're presenting and then remember it later, use simple pictures as part of your presentation.

Pictures are remembered better than words. Words and pictures together are remembered better still. The pictures don't have to be very elaborate: people seem to remember the outline of an image more than the details. But people interpret information more accurately and consistently if it is presented with a relevant illustration.

Can't I Just Use Clip Art for Everything?

The picture must be easy to recognize and must clarify the meaning of the idea you're trying to get across. It also has to be easy to draw, since you often can't find clip art that accurately represents the idea and is appropriate for your audience. For example, it's pretty silly to use clip art of a football team to represent teamwork if your audience is mostly women.

Plan your pictures first; then look for clip art that is really appropriate. Sometimes you can find a piece of clip art that is almost right, and modify it using a paint program (graphics software). If you can't find anything, it's much better to use a primitive drawing that helps the audience understand than a wonderful piece of clip art that misses the point.

USE A GRAPHICAL ALPHABET

You can use geometric shapes as building blocks for simple drawings, just like you build words out of letters. The shapes below are building blocks for drawings and are the key to "no talent" drawings. I learned this approach from David Sibbet of Grove Consultants.

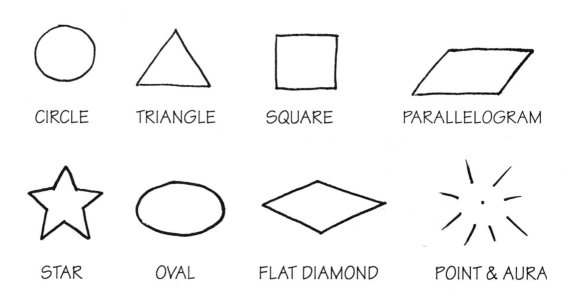

CIRCLE   TRIANGLE   SQUARE   PARALLELOGRAM

STAR   OVAL   FLAT DIAMOND   POINT & AURA

Use these shapes to create symbolic rather than realistic drawings—just as children and many artists do. The next few pages will show you how and give you some practice.

Use *Symbolic* Rather Than *Realistic* Drawings

- Saves Time
- Easier to Do
- Easier to Recognize

- Build "Graphic Vocabulary" Quickly
- Less Worry About "Drawing it RIGHT"

Kids' Stuff Is Best!

It's easy to recognize and remember, fast and easy to draw.

FACES: Circles, Lines and Dots

PROFILES

Circle and Cross-Hairs for Skull

Add Square for Chin

Add Triangle for Nose

Draw Outline in Ink

Play with Mouth, Eyes

 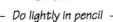 ── *Do lightly in pencil* ──

PEOPLE

VEHICLES & BUILDINGS

Car   Truck   House   Skyscrapers

Diamond Worksheet

Connect the dots to make 3 more diamonds:

Draw 3 more long, flat diamonds in this space:

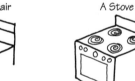

Remember the stack lines	First draw only horizontal lines	Then add vertical lines	Add doors & windows (follow the imaginary stack lines)
A gift	A Table	A Chair	A Stove

Turn these diamonds into something (and then go up to the diamonds you made above and make them into something):

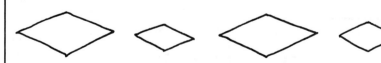

Draw!

Using geometric shapes as building blocks, draw some simple ideas and objects below.

1. Draw money. Try using a parallelogram with a dollar sign on it.

2. Turn it into a stack of money.

3. Turn it into runaway costs (legs? wheels? wings?).

4. Draw a personal computer. Try using squares for the CRT, and a parallelogram for the keyboard.

5. Add a mouse.

6. Draw a building. Try a diamond. Refer back to the diamond worksheet if you get lost.

 Use the next few pages to practice drawing people and faces. Then look at Pictograms and Ideograms for more ideas.

People Worksheet

Stick
Person

Star
Person

Speedo
Person

Big Foot
Person

Practice:

Male Faces Worksheet

| Face
Front | Simple
Profile | Lively
Profile | Smug
Profile | Beanhead:
Exaggerated
Features |

Practice:

42

Female Faces Worksheet

Face   Lively   Self-Satisfied   Distressed
Front   Profile

(Smaller features, eyelashes, more hair. Optional: Fuller lips, earrings.)

Practice:

Pictures of Things . . . Add Your Own!

Pictures of Ideas . . . Add Your Own!

After David Sibbet & Geoff Ball

More Useful Images

USING SIMPLE PICTURES

Here are some things to do to start putting simple pictures to work for you:

► Make a list of concepts that you frequently need to get across to others. To start with, list only concepts you can express in one to three words. Examples: budgeting, regulation, downsizing, acquisitions, values, paradigms, controlled growth, cycle time, time to market, product life cycle, education and diversity. We will deal with more complex, wordy concepts in the section on planning a presentation.

- Write each concept on a separate 3" × 5" card and arrange the cards in roughly priority order: the highest priority goes on top.

- Sit down with some colored felt pens, some scratch paper and your concept cards.

- Read your first card (say, "cost control") and take a piece of scrap paper to scribble down the ideas and images that "cost control" suggests to you. For example, to me it suggests money (a stack of dollar bills) and some control-related things like a leash, a rope, a net, a cage, a steering wheel and brakes.

- Now try drawing some of those images together on your scrap of paper. Do several until you find one that could work. Here's the best image I came up with for cost control:

- Copy your most promising image on the 3" × 5" card along with the concept name. Treat this as "clip art" for your own work; copy it onto your graphic next time you need to present this idea.

- Keep going until you have images for a least five concepts. If you get stuck thinking up an image for a card, set it aside for the next activity.

► Play Pictionary™ using the cards you couldn't think of images for, following the instructions on the next page.

WHERE DO YOU GET THE IDEAS?

Ideas for images come from your own imagination (as soon as you quit telling yourself you don't have any), from your friends, your colleagues, your audiences and your kids. Here's one of many ways to call images up and start building an image vocabulary and a picture file.

Here's How:

1. Make a list of ideas, facts, concepts and principles that you'd like to have images for. Don't hold back . . . nothing is impossible.

> **TIP:** Start carrying a few 3" × 5" cards around with you in your purse, pocket or briefcase and jot down things you'd like to illustrate as they occur to you.

2. Write each idea on a 3" × 5" card.

3. Get together with some people who will indulge in a little craziness with you:

   - Other people who have this book

   - Good friends in comfortable, social surroundings

   - Someone who already does good visuals or who paints, draws or doodles a lot

   - Someone who really likes computer graphics and plays with clip art

   - Any kids, anywhere

> **TIP:** People may have ideas they'd like images for, too . . . especially a group of colleagues. Give them 3" × 5" cards to write their ideas on and add them to your pile.

4. Shuffle the 3" × 5" cards and play some form of "pictionary":

- Classic Pictionary™ with teams and scores

- The version from the "Graphic For Presenters" workshop

  —you draw a card and read it

  —everyone draws an image on a piece of paper

  —everyone holds up their image at once to share ideas

- Or, invent your own version!

> **TIP:** Have everyone write the name of the idea next to their image.

5. Collect all the images and put them in an idea file until you're ready to make your visuals. Do thumbnail sketches first to test which images work best for you.

> **TIP:** If you have lots of images for each idea, set up a manila folder labeled with each idea and drop the sketches inside. Or at least staple them together. If people want to keep their sketches, photocopy them and keep the copies.
>
> Do this any time you need to prepare new visuals and are stuck for ideas.
>
> As long as you take time to plan an event that's fun or rewarding for people, they'll keep coming back to play. Over time, you'll acquire some wonderful resources and an extensive image vocabulary.
>
> You are always welcome to call me for ideas. I'm full of them. Lynn Kearny (510) 547–1896. Remember, I'm on Pacific Standard Time. Don't call at 5:00 A.M.!

P A R T

7

Putting It All Together

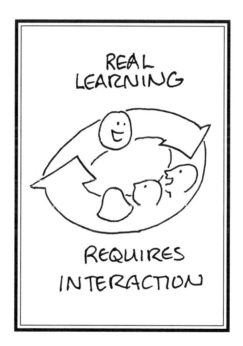

PUTTING IT ALL TOGETHER

Now it's time to put all the graphic elements together into one visual aid—in this case a flip chart or an overhead transparency.

First, here are some examples of visual aids made with five basic graphic elements: words and letters, blank space, lines and shapes, color and simple pictures. Since this book isn't printed in color, you'll have to imagine that part.

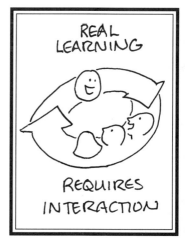

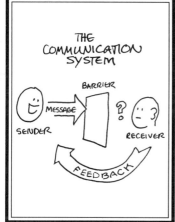

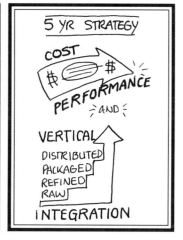

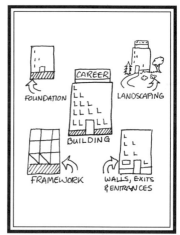

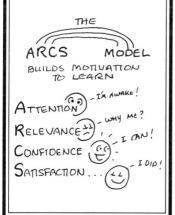

by John Keller,
Florida State University

Adapted from "The Northbound train" © 1994 Karl Albrecht Used with permission.

NOW IT'S YOUR TURN

Think of something you will present (or have presented) to others. It can be a concept, a list of guidelines or a set of instructions (like for a procedure or a classroom learning activity). Write its name in the space below:

_____

If you are unable to think of anything, present this concept:

> **The key to managing productivity is to balance staff availability with labor costs.**

- Quickly review the guidelines for words and letters.

Guidelines

► PRINT IN CAPS $1\frac{1}{2}$" HIGH

► ALTERNATE COLORS

► USE ONLY KEY WORDS

► LIST NO MORE THAN 5 IDEAS/PAGE

► LEAVE LOTS OF WHITE SPACE

- Use a blank sheet of flip-chart paper and colored felt-tipped markers. If you want to make an overhead instead, I suggest you do a rough draft on $8\frac{1}{2}$" × 11" paper first, using fine-tipped colored felt pens.

- Now create a visual aid for the topic you selected. (Allow yourself about 15–20 minutes for this.) It should include all five of the graphic elements:

  —words and letters

  —blank space

  —lines and/or geometric shapes

  —color

  —simple pictures

- When you are finished, tape it to a wall and take a short break. Then come back and review it with fresh eyes.

  —is it easy to read and understand quickly?

  —if it is something people need to remember, do you think remembering it will be easy?

  —even if the drawing isn't as professional as you would like, could someone else recognize what it is?

  —are the images big enough to be seen from the audience?

  —do you like it?

- If the answer to any of these questions is "no," review the preceding sections of the book and see if you can figure out how to fix your visual aid so the answer is "yes."

- If you have followed all the guidelines and you still aren't quite happy with the result, read the next section on composition.

P A R T

8

Composition

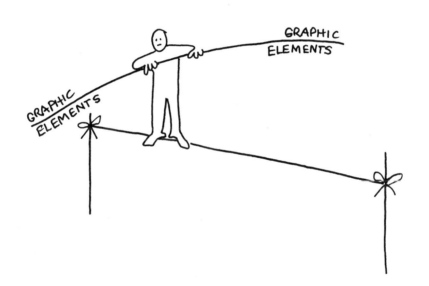

DOES IT LOOK RIGHT?

When we look at a visual, we may find it satisfying. Or, we might find it unsatisfying and not be sure why. Here's where your talent for noticing something's wrong will pay off. You already have all the skills you need to fix it—you only need a little knowledge.

Composition refers to how something is put together, and how its elements relate to each other. In the case of visuals, we're interested in the arrangement of graphic elements on the page. The two most important parts of composition for visual aids are focus and balance.

FOCUS

Focus is just what it sounds like: it means where you focus when you look at the visual. There's a problem if the eye doesn't know where to go, or if it focuses on something unimportant.

If you follow the guidelines for words and lettering and for using color, your visual should have no problems with focus.

When you're adding pictures, make sure images are about important ideas you want viewers to focus on and remember.

Example:

You want people to learn that during negotiation it's important to find out the other party's actual needs and try to satisfy their needs rather than their demands.

The pictures should be of *needs* versus *demands* (e.g., a life boat vs. a luxury liner). It should not be a picture of negotiators facing off across a table.

If a visual looks too crowded, it is. To restore focus, take out the guidelines sheet on page 13 and identify how to fix it.

- Which of these pages has good focus?

- What would improve the focus of the other?

- Use this blank box to re-do the problem page and give it focus.

BALANCE

Balance means that if you divided the page down the center, the graphic elements on both sides would look like they were in balance with each other.

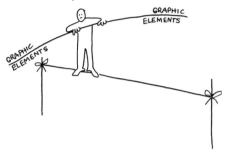

Neither side of the page would look lighter or heavier than the other.

Reminder: Graphic elements are:

- Words and letters
- Blank space
- Lines and shapes

- Color
- Simple pictures

Examples:

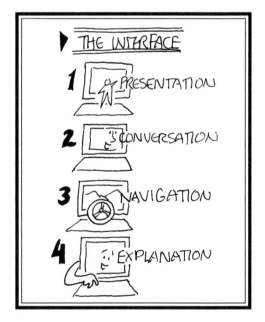

This page has good balance.

The balance here is not good: it looks like it would tip to the left.

WEIGHT

A graphic element can look heavy or light, which will affect the balance of a page. The chart below shows how to make an element appear heavy or light.

Two things that create the impression of balance are:

- Weight (how heavy an element looks)

- Placement (how far it is placed from the center)

HEAVY	LIGHT
DARK OR INTENSE COLOR	**LIGHT COLOR**
	SMALL
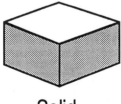 Solid Looking	 Detailed or Delicate Looking

WEIGHT (continued)

This cover sheet is balanced.

- The square is big, but it's a light color
- The triangle is small but it's very dark so it looks heavy

This cover sheet is not balanced.

- The letters are big and dark, so they look heavy
- The shapes are very small and light, so they don't "balance" the letters

This cover sheet is not balanced.
YOU TRY IT! . . .

Re-draw it here so it is in balance.

PLACEMENT

The further a design element is from the center, the more it seems to tip the page in its direction. This is just like putting a child on a teeter totter: if the child sits way out at the end he will tip his end more easily than if he were sitting in the middle of the board near the balance point. Look at the examples below:

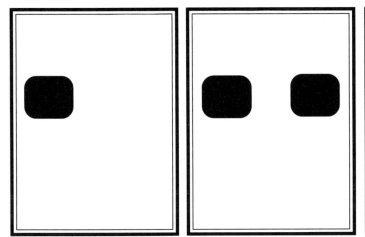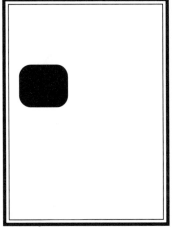

This element is placed so far left it makes the page look out of balance.

Add something that creates balance.

You try another way to create balance.

Practice

Play with this by cutting out different sizes and shapes of colored paper. Put "Tack-a-Note™" glue (by Dennison™) or "Dry Line™" (by Liquid Paper™) on their backs and play with re-arranging them on a blank flip chart. Then experiment by adding lettering.

PLACEMENT (continued)

Practice

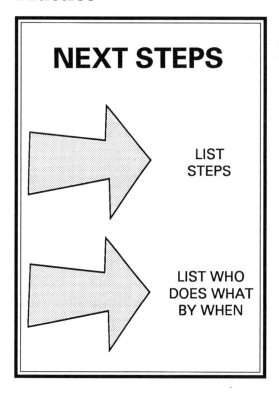

NEXT STEPS

LIST STEPS

LIST WHO DOES WHAT BY WHEN

INSTRUCTIONS

- **Answer p 59**

- **Work in pairs**
  -discuss
  -pick 3

- **Prepare to present**
  -flip chart
  -spokesperson

- **Time: 20 min.**

Application

Use these guidelines and examples to review and edit your own charts.

P A R T

9

Planning a Presentation

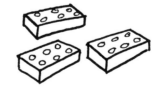

PULLING THE PIECES TOGETHER

This section will help you plan for a full presentation requiring a whole series of visual aids. Our focus in the book will be on preparing to teach a class, or to make a presentation to another kind of group. If you are designing a manual or a series of computer screens, you will go through a similar process. Although you may not have some of the same items (like an agenda), you will likely have something like a cover sheet (title screen) and you will certainly have lots of key concepts and instructions. You will find this approach useful if you are willing to be flexible and interpret these recommendations for your own situation.

This section will cover:

- Useful visuals

- Using thumbnail sketches to plan visuals

- Useful techniques for each type of visual

- How to work with complex, wordy material

- Tips for living (and traveling) with flip charts

USEFUL VISUALS

First, decide what parts of your class or presentation you would like to have visual aids for. Here is a list of the types of visuals I find useful every time I present:

- Cover sheet

- Objectives

- Agenda

- Key concepts

- Guidelines and other lists

- Instructions for exercises and activities

I go through my leader's guide or other presentation outline and mark down all the key concepts, guidelines and activities I will want visuals for.

You Try It

Choose a presentation you will soon have to give. If there isn't one, pick something you did in the not-so-distant past. You should take at least an hour's worth of presentation material.

Use the space below to list the general types of visuals you would like to have: cover sheet, agenda, etc.

Take your leader's guide, outline or any other presentation notes, and mark everything that you really want people to understand and remember. These will be the things to prepare visual aids for.

THUMBNAIL SKETCHES

Thumbnail sketches are miniature rough drafts you make of your visuals. The purpose of thumbnails is to let you work fast and rough without wasting time or materials on full-sized graphics until you know exactly what you want each one to look like.

If you are preparing visuals for someone else, thumbnails are a great timesaver. Use them to sketch out your ideas and get approval before you do the real ones. You can also try thumbnails out on one or two members of your target audience to find out whether the visuals help them understand and remember or not.

When you have your list of visuals (from the previous page), make several photocopies of the Thumbnail-Sketch Worksheet on page 70. You will use them along with some fine-tipped colored felt pens to start drawing miniature versions of your visual aids. Most of the illustrations and examples in this book are thumbnail versions of larger graphics.

When you have made your photocopies, read the guidelines on the following pages and start drawing your thumbnails.

Thumbnail-Sketch Worksheet

Use this sheet to plan your flip charts (or other visuals) before you do the full-sized ones. Use fine-tipped colored felt pens so you can see what the finished visual will look like. Work fast and rough.

USEFUL TECHNIQUES FOR COVER SHEETS AND AGENDAS

You already know all the techniques you need for making good cover sheets and agendas. Use:

- Guidelines for words and letters

- Your best and neatest lettering (more important on the first few sheets)

- Multicolored borders and interesting bullet points

- Color

For cover sheets, consider also using:

- Fancy lettering

- A very finished drawing or cartoon. (This is a good use for appropriate clip art.)

You Try It

Make thumbnail sketches of the cover sheet and agenda (if any) for the presentation you selected above. Use your fine-point colored felt pens and Thumbnail-Sketch Worksheets. Work fast and rough—if you don't like something, cross it out and try again.

TECHNIQUES FOR GUIDELINES AND OTHER LISTS

- Words and lettering

- Bullet points

- Color

- Simple pictures to help understand and remember items on the list

Example:

FLOWCHART GUIDELINES

1. FLOW LEFT TO RIGHT, → TOP TO BOTTOM ⇩

2. SPACE SYMBOLS AT AN □–◇–□–◇ EQUAL DISTANCE

3. AVOID CROSSING LINES

You Try It

Make thumbnail sketches of any guidelines or other lists for the presentation you are planning.

TECHNIQUES FOR GIVING INSTRUCTIONS:

- Pictures that show what to do

- Key words to clarify

Example:

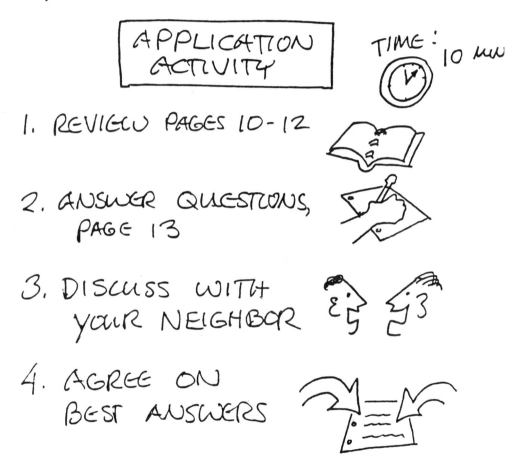

You Try It

Make thumbnail sketches of any instructions for procedures, exercises or activities in the presentation you are planning.

TECHNIQUES FOR KEY CONCEPTS

For key concepts, use:

- Guidelines for words and letters

- Bullet points

- Color

- Simple pictures

If the concept is complex and wordy, see the next topic on "chunking."

You Try It

Sketch thumbnails of some key concepts in the presentation you are planning. If any are very wordy or complex, look at the next topic first and then come back and finish your thumbnails.

CATABOLISM

CATABOLISM IS LIKE TAKING A "LEGO" STRUCTURE APART.

YOU START WITH SOMETHING COMPLEX

AND BREAK IT INTO COMPONENT PIECES

WHICH GET SMALLER AND SMALLER.

YOU END UP WITH A BUNCH OF SIMPLER PARTS THAT CAN BE USED AGAIN TO MAKE SOMETHING ELSE.

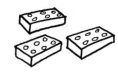

CHUNKING COMPLEX, WORDY MATERIAL

Some concepts aren't easily expressed in one to three words, or even five to ten words. And sometimes you need to help people grasp an idea that's very wordy indeed. Examples are corporate-mission or -vision statements, formal statements of objectives and many technical concepts. Here's an approach that is very effective for breaking down a key concept into manageable chunks and converting into visual language.

First, "chunk" the information by breaking it down into short, meaningful phrases of three to five words in length.

Example

The key to managing productivity is to balance staff availability with labor costs.

Chunked:

the key to managing
productivity

is to balance staff
availability

with labor costs

CHUNKING COMPLEX, WORDY MATERIAL (continued)

Second, rearrange it on the page, adding graphic elements to clarify the meaning, using ONLY key words.

You Try It

Take any complex, wordy material you ran into in the presentation you are planning. It may be a concept, an objective, a corporate vision statement or any really abstract idea.

- Use a piece of scratch paper to chunk it

- Think of simple pictures that help clarify the meaning of each chunk

- Rearrange the chunks on the page, adding pictures that clarify meaning

- If possible, add lines and shapes to help show how the chunks relate to each other (as in the example above)

It helps to think of the chunks as "eye bites," little bits of meaningful information that can be taken in and understood at a glance.

Once you have done this, CONGRATULATIONS! You have just completed the graduate exercise. There are lot of professional graphic artists who don't know how to do this.

FROM PLANNING TO PRODUCTION

You may want to do one last check and look at the composition of each thumbnail before you turn it into a full-sized graphic. Does it have focus? Does it look like it's about to tip in one direction, or is it balanced? Fix the thumbnail and re-draw it to make sure you're satisfied.

When you have thumbnails you are satisfied with for all the visual aids you need, go ahead and produce full-sized visuals. You will find the process a lot faster, as well as more satisfying and fun, if you have a set of thumbnails to work from. You can put all your energy and attention into being creative now that the planning is done. You will also find your visuals have more unity; they look like they belong together and they flow from one to the next.

The next few pages will give you tips for creating full-sized flip charts, assembling them, traveling with them and storing them.

TIPS FOR LIVING (AND TRAVELING) WITH FLIP CHARTS

Tip #1 One Sheet at a Time

► Create your visuals one sheet at a time. When a visual is complete, tear it off the pad and set it aside to be assembled later.

► Discard or retrace major goofs and sheets you just don't like.

► Do not try to create a complete flip chart pad of perfect visuals (no goofs allowed) and then try to cart the whole pad around, complete with cardboard backing. There are easier ways!

Tip #2 Use a Template

► Use a lined flip-chart pad to create a template. Create a border 2" to 3" deep all the way around one sheet. Then add horizontal lines for lettering guides. Using a yardstick and a blue marker, trace over every other line. Then using a red marker, trace over the lines in between.

► Slip this sheet under each new blank sheet of paper you're working on. Use it to:

  • keep your lines of lettering straight and even

  • keep your letters of uniform height (1" or 2" high)

  • keep your margins straight and clean

Tip #3 Assemble and Disassemble Charts

► Select each finished sheet you want to use for your next presentation.

► Stack each in order with a blank sheet between so you can't see the next sheet through it.

► Use two large paper clips to clip the stack of sheets together at the top: one clipped horizontally at the top left corner and one at the top right. This method will keep your sheets neat and compact until you need them.

► Hang two large binder clips from the pins at the top of your flip-chart stand.

Clip the assembled stack of visuals to these, and you're ready to present.

Tip #4 Preserve Your Work

► For visuals you post on classroom walls with tape, create a tape shield. Simply put a few strips of transparent tape in each top corner as a permanent shield. Drafting tape will stick to the surface, but can easily be removed without hurting the visual aid.

► For a paper flip-chart sheet that will see lots of use, protect all the edges with tape. Here's how:

- turn the sheet over and work on the back

- along each edge run a long strip of tape about 1/16" in from the edge

Tapes I use are:

► Scotch Magic Tape™ (3/4") or

► Scotchmark Paper Tape™ (3/4"). It's also called "artists' tape" and "white paper tape," and is available in art supply stores.

- tape all four edges of the sheet

- Trim off any tape that overlapped an edge to avoid visible, sticky edges. You now have a remarkably sturdy sheet that will not tear or get curly, dog-eared edges.

TIPS FOR LIVING (AND TRAVELING) WITH FLIP CHARTS (continued)

Tip #5 Travel with Flip Charts

► Transport the paper-clipped stacks by rolling them, starting from the clipped top. If you start at the bottom, they'll wrinkle or slip out of the clips.

► Wrap the roll(s) in large plastic trash bags, or have someone make you a fabric carrying case with handles.

► Lighten your load by removing all the blank sheets and carrying only the rolled visuals on the plane. This reduces weight by 50%. Phone ahead and ask your hotel to have a blank flip-chart pad waiting with the bell captain when you check in. (Remember that catering provides these pads in most hotels, and their office hours are only from 9:00 A.M. to 5:00 P.M. weekdays.) Simply tear blank sheets off the pad and slip them between your visuals, then replace the clips. After the presentation, remove and recycle the blanks.

Tip #6 Store Your Charts Neatly

► Stack chart sheets carefully after a presentation. Assemble the stack so no individual sheets have their edges sticking out of the pile. Remove the clips if you need to, then replace them. This prevents bent, dirty and raggedy edges.

► Store visuals you aren't using on a flat shelf or other surface. If you store them rolled, they get into the habit of curling and it's hard to retrain them.

WHAT'S NEXT?

You have all the basic skills you need to plan and prepare good, graphic visual aids for presenting ideas and information to other people. You will have a much greater impact now than you would have had without them. Your ideas will be understood and remembered by more people. Where can you go from here?

The back of this book has three sets of resources to pursue if you'd like to go further with graphics:

- A section of advanced techniques

- An expanded list of materials and supplies

- An annotated bibliography of more books on how to do graphics

Enjoy yourself and have fun!

10

Advanced Techniques

ADVANCED TECHNIQUES WITH WORDS AND LETTERS

Once you're comfortable with basic techniques with words and letters, try using fancy lettering.

If you are using a computer to create a flier, slides or overhead transparencies, you will have lots of fonts available to experiment with. I strongly recommend you don't try to use more than two or three fonts on a single visual aid or slide. Make sure they go together: they should look good and also look like they're related in some logical way. You don't want **Fancy Gothic Script** together with a font that looks like Handwriting and another that looks Exotic (example on the left). All your fonts should look like they're telling the same story (example on the right).

Headline	Headline
First Subhead	**First Subhead**
Body text could be like this.	Body text could be like this.

Avoid this mix of fonts. These fonts match better.

It's also important to pick fonts that are easy to read. If you're determined to use Gothic lettering on your flier make sure the words are familiar and easy to recognize, like "Merry Christmas."

If you are using flip charts, some techniques for fancy lettering are shown on the next few pages.

USE FANCY LETTERING

Use fancy lettering for key words on a chart, such as

- The title of the chart

- A key word (like "quality") that you really want to stand out

Try using:

Experiment with:

PUFFY LETTERS

- First sketch the letters in pencil

- Then fill them in with a colored highlighter (like pale blue or pale purple)

- Next outline them with a related dark-colored felt pen (like dark blue or purple)

Try using these letters and getting a hot effect (yellow, orange, red) or cold effect (blue highlighter, turquoise, dark blue). This technique is explained on pages 29–32 in this book.

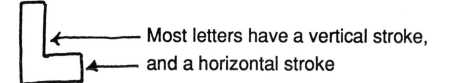

- First, draw the letters

- Then draw in the "shadow" on the side of each letter with another color of felt pen

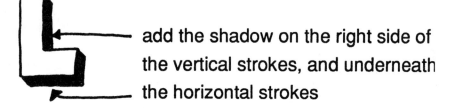

Most letters have a vertical stroke, and a horizontal stroke

add the shadow on the right side of the vertical strokes, and underneath the horizontal strokes

ADVANCED TECHNIQUES WITH LINES AND SHAPES

Lines

Try using lines to create an interesting page format that also helps organize information on the page. In the examples below, the same format has been used with several important flip-chart pages. This creates visual "unity" throughout the presentation. Unity means all the pieces look like they go together as part of a whole.

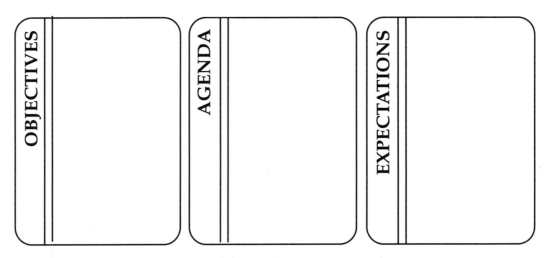

This also makes it easy for participants to see what each sheet is about, and leaves most of the space free for displaying actual information.

Geometric Shapes

Try using geometric shapes to make an interior "frame" that draws attention to an important word or idea. The frame also makes the page look more attractive and interesting. For example:

A Printed Handout

ADVANCED TECHNIQUES WITH COLOR

Add Emphasis

Here are some ways to add emphasis to a chart using color or lines. Note: Use only *one* technique on a visual, not all three.

- Print one or two key words in a hot color.

- Circle a key idea with yellow and create a yellow spotlight by coloring it in.

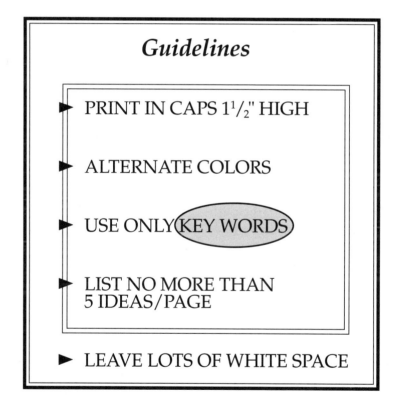

Guidelines

► PRINT IN CAPS 1¹/₂" HIGH

► ALTERNATE COLORS

► USE ONLY KEY WORDS

► LIST NO MORE THAN 5 IDEAS/PAGE

► LEAVE LOTS OF WHITE SPACE

- Use a highlighter and create an interior frame to emphasize an idea.

ADVANCED TECHNIQUES WITH COLOR (continued)

Hot Effects

Use if you want to grab attention or create an impression of heat, brilliance or intensity.

Examples:

- Hot seat
- News flash
- Take the heat
- Conflict
- Danger
- Attention!

How To

Use your yellow, orange, and red felt pens. The effect will be intensified if you add two more colors:

► An orange highlighter pen

► A dark red art store pen (for example, Stabilayout™)

1. Outline the basic shape or area with yellow, then color it in solid yellow.

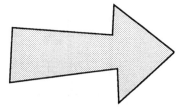

2. Outline the shape with your red pen (darkest red first).

3. Inside the red outline, do another outline with your next darkest pen. Use orange for this example.

The basic sequence is:

- Red (outside)

- Orange (middle)

- Yellow (inside)

The intensified version is:

- Dark Red (outside)

- Red

- Orange (middle)

- Orange Highlighter

- Yellow (inside)

Effect of Brilliance and Light

1. Leave the center of the shape or area plain white.

2. Color yellow away from the center (using a ray or sun-like effect) and end up with a wide area of yellow around the edges.

3. Then add the red and orange outlines on the outside of the figure only. Do not outline the hottest part of the flame at the center.

ADVANCED TECHNIQUES WITH COLOR (continued)

Cold Effects

Use if you want to create a cool, restful effect or an impression of coldness.

Examples:

- Cold calls
- Icebreaker
- Winter activity
- A cool response
- Cool-down period

How To

Use your dark blue, turquoise, and blue highlighter felt pens. Use the white of the paper as part of your color scheme.

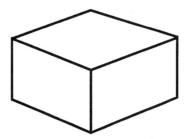

1. Outline the basic shape or area in dark blue.

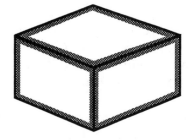

2. Inside the dark blue outline, do another outline with turquoise. Be sure to outline inside each part of the shape on all sides of the cube.

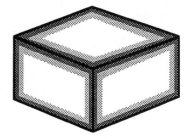

3. Inside the turquoise outline, do another outline with your blue highlighter. Leave the rest of the shape white.

If you have a complex chart and you want people to focus on a specific part, using light and dark felt pens will help.

- Use a dark-colored pen to draw and label the parts you want people to focus on

- Use a light-colored pen to draw everything else

Example:

On a cause-and-effect diagram, you want people to focus on the effect and on the names of the cause categories.

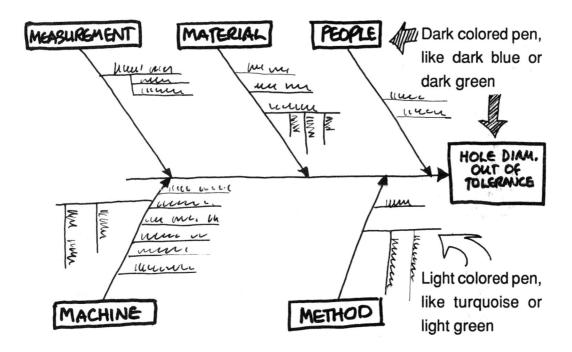

ADVANCED TECHNIQUES WITH SIMPLE PICTURES

You have already started drawing objects with a three-dimensional effect, that is, using depth. Geometric shapes helped:

parallelogram   diamond

You can add to that an impression of depth by using shading, overlap and varied sizes.

Shading

Imagine one side of your page to have a light source. When you draw objects, the shadow will always be on the side away from the light source.

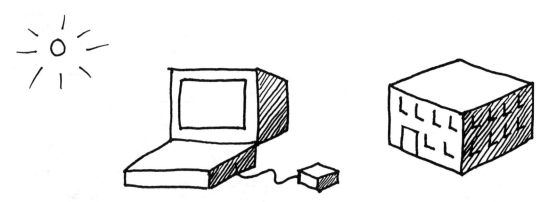

Add shading by:

- Making fine parallel lines in the same color

- By coloring in solids with a similar color highlighter

Depth

Now add a shadow to make the object appear to rest on a solid surface.

Draw short, parallel lines straight out to the side of the object. Put them only where the object would be resting on a surface.

TIP: Don't make a big dark, solid-looking shadow. Keep it small and light—just a suggestion of a shadow. Shadows in the real world are subtle. Study them.

Shading People

You can give faces and people an impression of depth and roundness by adding a light-toned pen inside the original outline.

Draw the person in brown pen.

Draw a light-brown* outline inside the dark brown one.

*Dilute a dry brown pen with injected water, or buy an art store pen like Stabilayout™.

ADVANCED TECHNIQUES WITH SIMPLE PICTURES (continued)

Overlap

You have already started using overlap to show depth. The keyboard overlaps the computer.

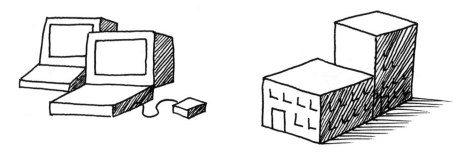

Draw a second object that appears to be behind the first—by using overlap.

- Draw a second object with its lines disappearing behind the first. Draw the second object in pencil, then add ink when it looks right.

- Draw the second object a little smaller. The second building is taller, but not as wide.

Try doing this yourself, below:

Size

Larger objects look closer than smaller objects.

Examples:

Which CRT looks
farther away?

Which person
looks closest?

Notice that the distant-
seeming objects are both
smaller and farther up on
the page.

Here both size and overlap
are being used to create an
impression of depth.

P A R T

11

More On Materials

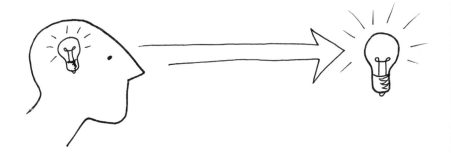

CREATING PAPER FLIP CHARTS

1. Paper

- Blank flip charts, also called easel pads

- Lined flip charts

- Grid-lined flip charts

- Butcher paper, in rolls of different widths. (Roll size is quoted in inches of width plus the weight of the roll, i.e., 30 lb. roll or 50 lb. roll.) This material is more economical, but less convenient. Consider buying a metal holder rack with a cutter, like the ones butchers have.

Sources: Office and art supply stores.
Paper-products supply houses (check the Yellow Pages™).

2. Tape

- Drafting tape is kindest to walls.

- Post-It™ Correction and Cover-up Tape (1" width) can be used to cover "goofs" so you can write over them again.

Sources: Art or drafting supply stores.
Any store where Post-It™ supplies are sold.

3. Pens

Use only water-based pens when working on paper. It washes off hands and clothing, and does not bleed through the paper onto furniture, walls or other graphics.

Best Kinds:

- Mr. Sketch™ (by Sanford)

Brown	Black
Purple	Red
Blue	Orange
Turquoise	Fuchsia
Dark Green	Yellow
Bright Green	

- Stabilayout™

  Grays
  Dark Red & Other Reds
  Aqua, Olive & Other Greens
  Light Brown
  Other Browns

CREATING PAPER FLIP CHARTS (continued)

3. **Pens (continued)**

Pens for Special Effects:

- Use Hi-Liter™ markers for creating space dividers, pale color areas or a 3-D effect:

  —a light blue (for depicting water or sheets of paper)

  —light green (for computer paper or grass)

  —light pink (for some flesh tones)

- Use a hypodermic full of water to dilute "dried out" Mr. Sketch™ pens and get paler colors:

  —light purple (for borders, underlines or shading)

  —light brown (for additional flesh tones or shading)

4. **Jazzy Stuff (use sparingly)**

- Use fluorescent highlighters to grab attention.

- Use gold notary stickers and large foil stick-on stars for bullet points.

- Look in art stores and office supply stores for other interesting and lively items such as special pens, stickers or templates.

Sources: Office supply stores.

5. **Fixing Goofs**

- Reusable surfaces you can write on:

  —white paper tape (by Post-It™)

  —large white paper labels

- Non-reusable surfaces:

  —Liquid Paper™ for pen and ink

Sources: Art and office supply stores.

CREATING PLASTIC FLIP CHARTS

1. Plastic Film

Translucent matte drafting film, .003 thickness:

- Single sheets

- Rolls of film

Sources: Art supply or drafting supply stores.

Note: Try to find rolls. Otherwise you may have to buy sheets larger than you actually want and cut them down. Duralene™, manufactured by Seth Cole™, can be used for this.

2. Plastic Flip-Chart Pads

"Static Images™" by 3M or "Wall Write™" by Permacharge™ are available through office supply stores. They may have to consult a supplier catalog and order it for you. Its features are:

- Opaque, white plastic sheets that do not require paper slip-sheets between them once inks are dry.

- Sheets that can be torn out of the pad and will adhere to most walls by static electricity alone (no tape needed).

- Sheets are washable.

- You can write on them with dry-erase markers and reuse them.

3. Pens

Use ONLY permanent pens when working on plastic. Take a strip of your plastic film with you to the art store and test each pen before you buy it: many colors look pale and weak on plastic film.

WORK IN A WELL-VENTILATED ROOM. The fumes from permanent pens are volatile and not healthy to breathe. Wear grubby clothing because stains do not come out.

CREATING PLASTIC FLIP CHARTS (continued)

3. Pens (continued)

Pens that test well: note: Try to find these brands. It's hard to find black, red, green or blue pens that look strong and clear on plastic film.

- <u>Carter's Marks-A-Lot</u>™
  - Brown
  - Green
  - Purple

- <u>Pilot Super Color Marker</u>™ (Broad)
  - Black
  - Red
  - Blue

Also very good are:

- Staedtler™ Lumocolor Permanent Overhead Transparency Markers (Extra Broad).

Black	Red
Blue	Brown
Green	Purple

These pens dry quickly, with none of the problems described on the following page. Their only drawback is the limited number of colors available.

<u>Pantone</u>™ pens by Letraset™, Broad Nib, and Permanent

Purples
266M (deep purple)
259   (red violet)

Blues
072M (deep blue)
293M (medium blue)
313M (blue green)

Hot Colors
206M (raspberry red)
032M (poppy red)
"Pantone Super Warm Red M"
   (orange)
137M (deep gold)

Browns
161M (soft brown)
160M (reddish-brown skin)
465M (Caucasian, Asian or
        Hispanic skin)

Black
"Pantone Extra Black M" (black)
"Cool Grey 11M" (grey)

Note: Most Pantone™ pens have numbers only, not names. My own descriptions of the colors are in parenthesis. Pantone browns and greens are weak and pale on plastic film. Therefore, it's best to use other brands except for skin colors.

4. Goofs

- Some errors with lighter-colored pens can be removed with a soft art eraser.

- Almost all mistakes can be removed with denatured alcohol on a cotton swab. Be careful—alcohol spreads much faster and farther than water. Don't let it destroy other parts of your graphic.

5. Beware!

Permanent inks on plastic take weeks, if not months, to dry completely. Here's how to handle them:

- Let the visual dry in open air without anything touching the ink for at least 12 hours. Hang it on the wall or in front of a window.

- Put paper slip-sheets between each visual or assemble them by taping them into a paper flip-chart pad. You can now use them.

- After a month or so, the paper will be spotty with blotted-up inks. Transfer the plastic charts to a fresh pad and it should stay clean.

If somehow the plastic charts end up getting stacked without paper, little blots of permanent ink will get deposited on the back of each chart. DON'T PANIC! Simply wipe the back of the chart clean with denatured alcohol, then restack with fresh paper between each set. (Staedtler™ Lumocolor Transparency Markers do not have these drying problems.)

6. Test Your Visuals First

Make your visuals on paper first and try them out a few times. Modify them until you're satisfied. Then trace them onto plastic, creating a permanent set. This will save time and hassle in the long run.

PART

12

Bibliography

CARTOONING AND DRAWING HOW-TO BOOKS

CARTOONING
By Hal Tollison
Published by Walter Foster Publishing
430 West Sixth Street
Tustin, California 92680

DRAWING FOR OLDER CHILDREN & TEENS
By Mona Brookes, 1991
Published by Jeremy P. Tarcher/Parigee

ED EMBERLEY'S DRAWING BOOK: MAKE A WORLD
and ED EMBERLEY'S DRAWING BOOK OF FACES
Both by Ed Emberley, Published by Little, Brown and Company

These simple books show how to draw thousands of things and people, using just a few geometric shapes, and dots and lines. A wonderful resource for people who believe they can't draw. Biggest bonus: everything's quick to draw and easy to understand.

FUNDAMENTALS OF GRAPHIC LANGUAGE: PRACTICE BOOK
and I SEE WHAT YOU MEAN: AN INTRODUCTION TO GRAPHIC
LANGUAGE RECORDING AND FACILITATION
Both by David Sibbet
Published by Grove Consultants International
832 Folsom Street, Suite 810
San Francisco, California USA 94107
(415) 882-7760

MARK KISTLER'S DRAW SQUAD
By Mark Kistler, 1988
A Fireside Book published by Simon & Schuster Inc.

THE BIG YELLOW DRAWING BOOK
By Dan O'Neil, Marion O'Neil and Hugh D. O'Neil, Jr.
Published by Hugh O'Neil & Associates
Nevada City, California

A workbook emphasizing the basic principles of learning, teaching and drawing through cartooning.

CARTOONING AND DRAWING
HOW-TO BOOKS (continued)

THE BOOK OF GRAPHIC PROBLEM-SOLVING: HOW TO
GET VISUAL IDEAS WHEN YOU NEED THEM
By John Newcomb
Published by R. R. Bowker Company
245 West 17th Street, New York, New York 10011

This is a wonderful resource for someone who often needs to come up with ideas to illustrate concepts: for training visuals, newsletter illustrations, etc. It teaches a step-by-step method for generating lots of on-target image ideas.

RAPID VIZ: A NEW METHOD FOR THE
RAPID VISUALIZATION OF IDEAS
By Hanks and Bellison
Published by Crisp Publications
1200 Hamilton Court
Menlo Park, California 54025
(650) 323-6100

BOOKS ON DESIGN AND LAYOUT

NOTES ON GRAPHIC DESIGN AND VISUAL COMMUNICATION
By Gregg Berryman
Published by Crisp Publications
1200 Hamilton Court
Menlo Park, California 54025
(650) 323-6100

HOW TO UNDERSTAND AND USE DESIGN AND LAYOUT
By Alan Swann
Published by North Light Books
1507 Dana Avenue
Cincinnati, Ohio 45207
1 (800) 289-0963

Good for educating your eye on visual balance and composition. Contains good ideas for arranging lettering and pictures on the graphic arts.

PICTURE THIS: PERCEPTION & COMPOSITION
By Molly Bang
Published by Bullfinch Press; Little, Brown and Company, Inc. USA

ILLUSTRATING COMPUTER DOCUMENTATION: THE ART OF PRESENTING INFORMATION GRAPHICALLY IN PAPER AND ONLINE
By William Horton, 1991
Published by John Wiley & Sons, Inc. USA

Outstanding resource on all aspects of illustrating text. All recommendations are based on research in fields of cognitive psychology and perceptual psychology. The book is a very well organized and specific how-to manual that applies to illustrating all subjects, not just computer documentation.

NOTES

NOTES

NOTES

NOW AVAILABLE FROM
CRISP PUBLICATIONS

Books • Videos • CD Roms • Computer-Based Training Products

If you enjoyed this book, we have great news for you. There are over 200 books available in the *50-Minute*™ Series. To request a free full-line catalog, contact your local distributor or Crisp Publications, Inc., 1200 Hamilton Court, Menlo Park, CA 94025. Our toll-free number is 800-442-7477. Visit our website at http://www.crisp-pub.com.

Subject Areas Include:

Management

Human Resources

Communication Skills

Personal Development

Marketing/Sales

Organizational Development

Customer Service/Quality

Computer Skills

Small Business and Entrepreneurship

Adult Literacy and Learning

Life Planning and Retirement

CRISP WORLDWIDE DISTRIBUTION

English language books are distributed worldwide. Major international distributors include:

ASIA/PACIFIC

Australia/New Zealand: In Learning, PO Box 1051 Springwood QLD, Brisbane, Australia 4127
Telephone: 7-3841-1061, Facsimile: 7-3841-1580   ATTN: Messrs. Gordon

Singapore: Graham Brash (Pvt) Ltd. 32, Gul Drive, Singapore 2262
Telephone: 65-861-1336, Facsimile: 65-861-4815   ATTN: Mr. Campbell

CANADA

Reid Publishing, Ltd., Box 69559-109 Thomas Street, Oakville, Ontario Canada L6J 7R4.
Telephone: (905) 842-4428, Facsimile: (905) 842-9327   ATTN: Mr. Reid

Trade Book Stores: Raincoast Books, 8680 Cambie Street, Vancouver, British Columbia, Canada V6P 6M9.
Telephone: (604) 323–7100, Facsimile: 604-323-2600   ATTN: Ms. Laidley

EUROPEAN UNION

England: Flex Training, Ltd. 9-15 Hitchin Street, Baldock, Hertfordshire, SG7 6A, England
Telephone: 1-462-896000, Facsimile: 1-462-892417   ATTN: Mr. Willetts

INDIA

Multi-Media HRD, Pvt., Ltd., National House, Tulloch Road, Appolo Bunder, Bombay, India 400-039
Telephone: 91-22-204-2281, Facsimile: 91-22-283-6478   ATTN: Messrs. Aggarwal

MIDDLE EAST

United Arab Emirates: Al-Mutanabbi Bookshop, PO Box 71946, Abu Dhabi
Telephone: 971-2-321-519, Facsimile: 971-2-317-706   ATTN: Mr. Salabbai

SOUTH AMERICA

Mexico: Grupo Editorial Iberoamerica, Serapio Rendon #125, Col. San Rafael, 06470 Mexico, D.F.
Telephone: 525-705-0585, Facsimile: 525-535-2009   ATTN: Señor Grepe

SOUTH AFRICA

Alternative Books, Unit A3 Sanlam Micro Industrial Park, Hammer Avenue STRYDOM Park, Randburg, 2194 South Africa
Telephone: 2711 792 7730, Facsimile: 2711 792 7787   ATTN: Mr. de Haas